The series "XIII" was created by WILLIAM VANCE and

I.JIGOUNOV · Y.SENTE

RETURN TO GREEN FALLS

XIII

Colours: Bérengère Marquebreucq

9th CINEBOOK
The 9th Art Publisher

SECOND CYCLE – PREVIOUSLY IN *XIII*

After the failure of the coup attempt by the American far right – which the media will remember as the Conspiracy of the XX – and the death or arrest of those responsible, Jason McLane, also known as 'the amnesic Number XIII', is finally free to focus on healing.

Despite his investigations and the various encounters that have allowed him to learn much about his past, he still hasn't recovered his memory. Psychiatrist Nathan Lipsky had warned him before being murdered: his amnesia would only disappear once he let himself face the 'key, most likely painful, moments' of his past.

What tragedy could be worse than everything XIII has been through – so traumatic that it is still keeping him locked in his own mental prison?

Hoping to return to a 'normal life', Jason picks a new psychiatrist in the city nearest to Bar Harbor, Augusta. Dr Suzanne Levinson confirms her deceased colleague's diagnosis … but most importantly, she also tells her patient about a new brain stimulation technique that could help him in his quest.

That is when XIII's life begins to spiral out of control once again. A mysterious woman named Julianne insists on recruiting him into the ranks of USafe, a private security company. Jason is accused of the murder of two of his fisherman friends. The penitentiary where the last living members of the 'XX' were held in isolation is blown up with no survivors. And Colonel Jones, deployed in Afghanistan, is abducted by a group of Taliban in cahoots with some senior US officers…

XIII quickly realises that all these events are linked … and that the ultimate goal of whoever is orchestrating things is to get their hands on him!

At the same time, modern medicine succeeds in unveiling a corner of his memory, and an unknown aspect of his past emerges, apparently tied to the famous *Mayflower*.

How is he connected to one of the founding tales of his country? Why are the killers of the remarkably low-profile Mayflower Foundation hunting him – without trying to kill him? What do these people want from him?

Who is he that he hasn't found out yet?

The Day of the *Mayflower*

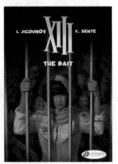

The Bait

Original title: Retour à Greenfalls
Original edition: © Dargaud Benelux (Dargaud-Lombard s.a.) 2013
by Sente & Jigounov
www.dargaud.com
All rights reserved
English translation: © 2016 Cinebook Ltd
Translator: Jerome Saincantin
Lettering and text layout: Design Amorandi
Printed in Spain by EGEDSA
This edition first published in Great Britain in 2016 by
Cinebook Ltd
56 Beech Avenue
Canterbury, Kent
CT4 7TA
www.cinebook.com
A CIP catalogue record for this book
is available from the British Library
ISBN 978-1-84918-301-7

9th CINEBOOK
The 9th Art Publisher

EASTERN AFGHANISTAN, AUTONOMOUS REGION OF BANICHISTAN...

I EXPECTED YOU WOULD REFUSE TO COOPERATE, MR MCLANE.

YOU AND YOUR FRIENDS ARE WILLING TO SACRIFICE YOUR LIVES. I DO NOT DOUBT IT. BUT PERHAPS NOT THE LIVES OF INNOCENT CITIZENS...

TO PASS THE TIME, I PROPOSE WE PLAY SOME DARTS.

LADIES FIRST. COLONEL JONES, YOU WILL HAVE THE FIRST MOVE. AIM FOR THE US ON THIS MAP.

YOU'RE EVEN CRAZIER THAN I THOUGHT. DARTS? WHAT ON EARTH DO YOU WANT ME TO...?

THROW!

3

NICE THROW, COLONEL! IT LOOKS LIKE YOU PICKED ... HARRISVILLE, MISSISSIPPI!

THANKS TO YOU, IN A COUPLE OF DAYS...

...THE ENTIRE WORLD WILL BE TALKING ABOUT THAT BACKWATER TOWN. I GUARANTEE THAT.

JUST AS I GUARANTEE THAT YOU WILL BE READY TO COOPERATE AFTERWARDS.

BANG

PUBLIC SCHOOL BANG

BANG BANG...

HEY! IT'S DONE! WHAT ARE YOU WAITING FOR? TIME TO SPLIT!

GOOD JOB! YOUR CASH AND YOUR DOPE ARE IN THE CAR. FIRST WE'VE GOT TO GET RID OF THE WEAPON, THOUGH...

...YES, ARMAND... TO BERNARD, AT THE PRÉSEAU-BAILLY POST OFFICE, THAT'S RIGHT... INSIDE HIS LETTER WILL BE ANOTHER ONE FOR YOU, WITH A MEMORY CARD YOU MUST PUT IN THE SAFE... WHAT WAS THAT?...

I KNOW THAT YOU USED TO BE A SPAD, MY DEAR, BUT STILL, DO BE CAREFUL... BECAUSE I LOVE YOU, OF COURSE... YES! SEE YOU SOON.

...THE INVESTIGATION IS JUST STARTING. SO FAR, THE DEATH TOLL STANDS AT TEN CHILDREN AND THE BUS DRIVER. THE SHOOTER KILLED HIMSELF AFTERWARDS. THE POLICE ARE CALLING FOR ANY WITNESSES TO...

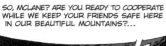

SO, MCLANE? ARE YOU READY TO COOPERATE WHILE WE KEEP YOUR FRIENDS SAFE HERE IN OUR BEAUTIFUL MOUNTAINS?...

...OR WOULD YOU RATHER WE PLAY ANOTHER ROUND OF DARTS?

MR MALLOCK? NUMBER XIII HAS JUST AGREED TO COOPERATE AT LAST!

...MALLOCK HERE. YOU CAN START THE REPATRIATION PROCEDURE, MR SHEPHERD.

LIEUTENANT COLONEL HAX? ELLERY SHEPHERD. SEND A TEAM TO ZONE D. THE PACKAGE WILL BE READY IN SIX HOURS.

GET A TEAM OF 'OUR' GUYS TOGETHER. A PACKAGE TO PICK UP AT POINT A4-27-28 IN SIX HOURS.

DAVID RIGBY?

THAT'S ME. MS BETTY BARNOWSKY, I PRESUME?

...OF COURSE I BELIEVE YOU! THERE'S NO WAY I CAN PICTURE JASON MCLANE BLOWING UP THAT PRISON IN THE PAINTED DESERT*. BUT YOU SEEM TO KNOW A LOT MORE ABOUT HIM THAN I DO. WHAT CAN I HELP YOU WITH?

JASON WON'T BE FREE UNTIL HE'S RECOVERED HIS MEMORIES AND SETTLED HIS ACCOUNTS WITH HIS PAST. BUT SO MUCH IS STILL HIDDEN IN THE DETAILS, MR RIGBY... HAVE YOU HAD TIME TO SORT THROUGH YOUR FILES?

HERE'S WHAT I FOUND. BUT I'LL ONLY LET YOU READ THEM IF YOU CALL ME DAVID!

THANK YOU ... DAVID. WE KNOW, THROUGH ZEKE HATTAWAY'S JOURNAL, THAT JONATHAN MCLANE WOULD LEAVE HIS HOME FOR A FEW DAYS EVERY MONTH. WE'RE TRYING TO FIGURE OUT WHERE HE WAS GOING, AND ESPECIALLY **WHOM** HE WAS MEETING.

I DON'T HAVE A BLESSED CLUE.

LET ME THINK, THOUGH... JONATHAN ALWAYS TRAVELLED BY BUS. AND THERE WAS ONLY ONE THAT WENT THROUGH GREEN FALLS. THE DRIVER LIVED THERE. YOU COULD OFTEN FIND HIM AT THE SEAVIEW BAR IN THE EVENING AFTER HE'D FINISHED WORK...

THAT'S A GREAT LEAD! DO YOU REMEMBER THAT DRIVER'S NAME?

NO, I'M SORRY... BUT ODDS ARE THAT JUDITH WILL.

JUDITH?

JUDITH WARNER, WHO USED TO BE GREEN FALLS' PHARMACIST. LET'S SAY SHE WAS WELL ACQUAINTED WITH MOST OF THE MEN IN AND AROUND TOWN. AND THE ONE THING I DO REMEMBER IS THAT THE DRIVER WAS RATHER A HANDSOME MAN...

*SEE VOLUME 19: *THE DAY OF THE MAYFLOWER*.

YOUR ANALYTICAL SKILLS ARE IMPRESSIVE, MY DEAR DAVID!

I'VE HONED MY JOURNALISTIC REFLEXES SINCE I'VE BEEN WORKING AT THE *SAN FRANCISCO CHRON-ICLE*. IT'S A BIG CHANGE FROM THE *MOUNTAIN NEWS*, BELIEVE ME.

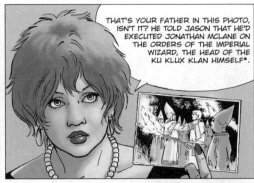

THAT'S YOUR FATHER IN THIS PHOTO, ISN'T IT? HE TOLD JASON THAT HE'D EXECUTED JONATHAN MCLANE ON THE ORDERS OF THE IMPERIAL WIZARD, THE HEAD OF THE KU KLUX KLAN HIMSELF*.

THAT'S HIM, YES. AND I'M NOT PROUD OF IT.

WOULD YOU MIND IF I TOOK THESE PICTURES? I'D APPRECIATE JUDITH WARNER'S ADDRESS, TOO, IF YOU HAVE IT.

THEY'RE ALL YOURS. I DON'T EVEN KNOW WHY I KEPT THEM... AS FOR JUDITH, SHE RUNS A DRUGSTORE IN SANTA MONICA. I'LL WRITE THE ADDRESS DOWN FOR YOU.

ARE YOU SURE YOU MUST LEAVE ALREADY? I'D BE HAPPY TO OFFER YOU DINNER.

MY DUCAL HUSBAND IS INSANELY JEALOUS, DAVID! JOKING ASIDE, I'M GOING TO FIND A MOTEL AND CRASH. I'M LEAVING EARLY TOMORROW. THANKS AGAIN.

OF COURSE YOU'RE MARRIED, BETTY. ANY WOMAN I FIND ATTRACTIVE IS MARRIED ... OR HER NAME IS JUDITH WARNER...

*SEE VOLUME 7: *THE NIGHT OF AUGUST THIRD*.

FBI REGIONAL HEADQUARTERS, BOSTON...

AGENT DODSON! WE'VE GOT A PING ON BETTY BARNOWSKY'S CREDIT CARD!

FINALLY!

SHE JUST RENTED A CAR FROM RENT-A-LUX IN SAN FRANCISCO!

I'LL CALL THEM.

...THAT'S RIGHT. A REDHEAD, KINDA PRETTY. I... SORRY?... SANTA MONICA, I RECKON, SINCE SHE ASKED US WHERE OUR BRANCH THERE IS.

CALL THE SANTA MONICA POLICE. GIVE THEM THE DESCRIPTION OF THE GIRL AND THE CAR, AND TELL THEM WE'RE ON OUR WAY!

7

9

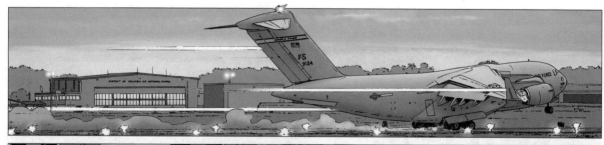

NOT THIS ONE, FELLAS. I HAVE TO TAKE HIM FOR AN AUTOPSY. THE AMBULANCE SHOULD BE HERE ANY MINUTE.

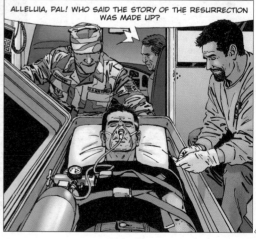

ALLELUIA, PAL! WHO SAID THE STORY OF THE RESURRECTION WAS MADE UP?

SORRY I COULDN'T INVITE YOU TO TRAVEL ABOARD MY JET, MCLANE. BUT WE WANTED TO AVOID PROBLEMS AT CUSTOMS — WHAT WITH YOU BEING ON THE MOST WANTED LIST AND ALL...

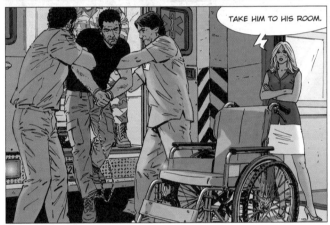

TAKE HIM TO HIS ROOM.

COME IN. LET ME INTRODUCE DR LEVINSON. THE SURGEON FROM WHOM YOU STOLE WALLY SHERIDAN'S MEDICAL FILE*. I'M SURE YOU REMEMBER THAT.

LEVINSON?!...

LET'S CLEAR UP ANY CONFUSION. THERE ARE TWO DR LEVINSONS. THE FATHER, AND HIS PSYCHIATRIST DAUGHTER, WHOM YOU ALREADY KNOW.

I... I'M SORRY...

COME NOW, SUZANNE! WHY APOLOGISE? YOU'RE HERE TO LET US EXPLORE OUR GUEST'S MEMORY UNDER THE BEST OF CONDITIONS, REMEMBER?

*SEE VOLUME 8: *THIRTEEN TO ONE*.

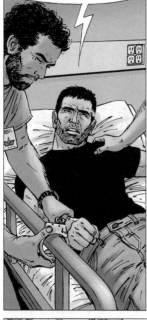

YOU'RE A COMPLETE PSYCHO! HOW COULD YOU SACRIFICE THOSE INNOCENT CHILDREN IN HARRISVILLE?!

THE REAL MADMEN IN THIS COUNTRY REGULARLY SLAUGH-TER PEOPLE WITH THE SOLE INTENT OF VENTING THEIR FRUSTRATIONS BEFORE KILLING THEMSELVES. COWARDLY, POINTLESS ACTS...

AT LEAST THE SACRIFICE OF THOSE YOUNG MARTYRS SERVED A PURPOSE: CONVINCING YOU TO COLLABORATE, MR MCLANE. GOD WON'T FORGET THEM.

LET'S BE PRAGMATIC. YOU AND I HAVE AN EQUALLY VESTED INTEREST IN SEEING YOU RECOVER YOUR MEMORIES. YOU, SO YOU CAN REBUILD A 'NORMAL' LIFE. ME... I'M GOING TO EXPLAIN WHY.

YOU'VE HEARD OF THE JOURNEY OF THE *MAYFLOWER* AND THE PILGRIM FATHERS, I'M SURE...

HOWEVER, BEHIND THE EDITED VERSION TAUGHT IN SCHOOLS IS ANOTHER STORY – ONE THAT FEW PEOPLE KNOW... IT BEGINS IN CENTRAL ENGLAND AT THE END OF THE 16TH CENTURY, IN THE VILLAGE OF SCROOBY.

THERE, PASTOR JOHN ROBINSON LOOKED AFTER THE FAITH OF A SMALL, SEPARATIST CONGREGATION OF PURITANS LED BY WILLIAM BREWSTER.

PERSECUTED BY THE ANGLICAN AUTHORITIES OF ENGLAND, OVER HALF OF THE CONGREGATION DECIDED TO FLEE TO THE NETHERLANDS IN 1608. THEY SETTLED IN LEIDEN TO START A NEW LIFE.

TEN YEARS LATER, JUDGING THE INFLUENCE OF DUTCH LIBERALISM DANGEROUS TO THEIR CHILDREN, THE CONGREGATION DECIDED TO LEAVE FOR THE NEW WORLD. THERE, AWAY FROM EVERYTHING AND EVERYONE, THEY WOULD BE FREE TO BUILD AN UNCORRUPTED COMMUNITY.

THE LEADER OF OUR ANCESTORS, WILLIAM BREWSTER, SIGNED A CONTRACT WITH THOMAS WESTON, AN ENGLISH MERCHANT REPRESENTING THE LONDON COMPANY. IT WOULD BRING THE SMALL PARTY TO THE LUSH COAST OF VIRGINIA SO THAT THEY COULD FOUND A COLONY THERE.

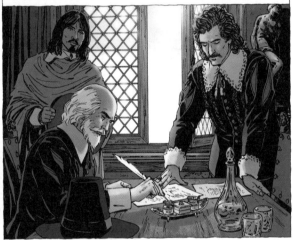

IN EXCHANGE, THE SETTLERS AGREED TO GIVE THE COMPANY THE PRODUCT OF FIVE DAYS A WEEK OF THEIR WORK FOR SEVEN YEARS, AFTER WHICH THEY WOULD BECOME MASTERS OF THEIR OWN FATE.

WESTON, HOWEVER, HAD 'FORGOTTEN' TO TELL THE PURITANS THAT THEY WOULDN'T BE ALONE ON THE TRIP. ALONG WITH THE *SPEEDWELL*, WHICH WAS TO BRING THE LEIDEN GROUP, ANOTHER SHIP, THE *MAYFLOWER*, WAS TO TRANSPORT SOME ENGLISH MERCHANT ADVENTURERS.

TOLD TOO LATE, AND HAVING ALREADY SOLD THEIR POSSESSIONS, OUR ANCESTORS HAD LITTLE CHOICE BUT TO ACCEPT THIS FORCED UNION. ON JULY 22, 1620, THE *SPEEDWELL* LEFT DELFSHAVEN TO JOIN THE *MAYFLOWER* IN SOUTHAMPTON.

11

FROM THE FIRST MEETING OF THE TWO GROUPS IN THE ENGLISH PORT, THE ADVENTURERS – THE STRANGERS – REVEALED THEIR ARROGANCE. THEY DEMANDED THE LEADERSHIP OF THE FUTURE COLONY. EVER MINDFUL OF RESPECTING OTHERS, THE PURITANS PROMISED TO DISCUSS IT...

SHORTLY AFTER DEPARTING, THE *SPEEDWELL* BEGAN TO TAKE ON WATER, FORCING BOTH SHIPS TO TURN BACK TWICE IN ORDER TO REPAIR THE DAMAGE SAFE IN THE ENGLISH PORT OF PLYMOUTH.

AND WHEN THE *SPEEDWELL* WAS JUDGED TOO UNTRUSTWORTHY FOR THE LONG JOURNEY, THOSE WHO DID NOT GIVE UP THEIR PLANS TRANSFERRED TO THE *MAYFLOWER*. ON SEPTEMBER 16, 1620, THE SHIP LEFT ENGLAND FOR GOOD.

UNFORTUNATELY, THE CROSSING WAS PLAGUED BY MORE AND MORE PROVOCATIONS FROM THE STRANGERS.

THE SITUATION DEGENERATED QUICKLY. FOOD WAS SCARCE. DISEASE WAS RAMPANT... EVENTUALLY, THE MEN CAME TO BLOWS!

THE LAST STRAW CAME WHEN A STORM PUSHED THE OLD SHIP AWAY FROM VIRGINIA AND TOWARDS THE COAST OF NEW ENGLAND INSTEAD. WINTER HAD ARRIVED IN FULL FORCE, AND EVERYONE WAS STARVING AND DISPIRITED. THE LEADER OF THE STRANGERS DECIDED TO END THE JOURNEY.

IN ORDER TO HAVE A CHANCE AT SURVIVING THE NATIVES AND HOSTILE ELEMENTS, THE TWO GROUPS HAD TO COME TO A PEACEFUL ARRANGEMENT.

THAT IS HOW, IN HIS GREAT WISDOM, OUR LEADER WILLIAM BREWSTER WROTE THE CHARTER THAT HISTORY WOULD REMEMBER AS THE MAYFLOWER COMPACT. BY THIS DOCUMENT, BOTH GROUPS AGREED TO FOLLOW RULES OF LIVING THAT WERE FAIRLY SIMILAR TO THOSE IN EXISTENCE IN MOST ENGLISH VILLAGES AT THE TIME.

HE THEN ASKED THE LEADER OF THE STRANGERS TO SIGN IT. THAT MAN'S NAME WAS CHRISTOPHER MARTIN... **YOUR ANCESTOR**, MR MCLANE.

THE ORIGINAL OF THE MAYFLOWER COMPACT WAS LOST. ALL WE HAVE IS THE LATER VERSION – CENSORED BY THE STRANGERS – BY WILLIAM BRADFORD IN HIS FAMOUS 1647 JOURNAL OF *PLYMOUTH PLANTATION*.

WE ALSO KNOW, THROUGH A DOCUMENT LITTLE KNOWN TO HISTORIANS, THAT THE COMPACT WAS SUPPLEMENTED WITH ANOTHER CONTRACT OF A MORE FINANCIAL NATURE BETWEEN THE TWO GROUPS. ITS MAIN PROVISION WAS FOR THE EQUAL AND COMPLETE SHARING OF ALL THE WEALTH PRODUCED BY EITHER SIDE IN THE NEW COLONY, FOR THE NEXT 400 YEARS.

IT WAS DECIDED THAT IN EACH SUCCEEDING GENERATION, THE LEADER OF EACH GROUP WOULD DESIGNATE HIS SUCCESSOR, AS WELL AS A 'GODFATHER' WHO WOULD SEE TO IT THAT THE NEW LEADER RESPECTED THE TERMS OF THE MAYFLOWER COMPACT AND THE FINANCIAL AGREEMENT. EVERYONE SIGNED THE ACCORDS, APPARENTLY WITH ENTHUSIASM.

BUT AFTER THE *MAYFLOWER* RETURNED TO ENGLAND, TENSIONS BETWEEN THE GROUPS REAPPEARED. THE MERCHANT ADVENTURERS THREATENED THE PURITANS' LIVES TO GET THEM TO RENOUNCE, IN WRITING, THE CONTRACT GUARANTEEING EQUITABLE SHARE OF THE INCOME.

MY ANCESTORS WERE FORCED TO SIGN AN ACT OF RENUNCIATION, THUS ABANDONING THEIR RIGHTS. WE HAD NOTHING LEFT BUT OUR FAITH ... AND OUR THIRST FOR REPARATION.

DURING THE FOLLOWING CENTURIES, OUR NEW LEADERS REFUSED TO GIVE IN AND KEPT WATCH OVER THE DESCENDANTS OF THE STRANGERS' LEADERS. ONE AFTER ANOTHER, THEY HOPED TO FIND WHERE THE ACT OF RENUNCIATION WAS HIDDEN. TO NO AVAIL.

OUR LAST HOPE VANISHED IN 1847. JAMES DUNCAN, THE LAST KNOWN LEADER OF THE MERCHANT ADVENTURERS, DIED IN A BOATING ACCIDENT IN GALWAY HARBOUR, IN IRELAND, ALONG WITH HIS GODFATHER.

HE LEFT NO DIRECT HEIR, NOR ANY INDICATION OF WHERE HE MIGHT HAVE HIDDEN THE PRECIOUS CONTRACT.

ANOTHER CENTURY AND A HALF WENT BY UNTIL MY PARENTS REVEALED TO ME THE HISTORICAL TRUTH ABOUT YOUR ANCESTORS' TREACHERY. I CONSULTED WITH THE BEST LAWYERS, WHO ALL CONFIRMED THAT WITHOUT THE ORIGINAL COMPACT AND FINANCIAL CONTRACT, WE HAD NO HOPE OF OBTAINING COMPENSATION. WE'D ALL BUT ACCEPTED THE VAGARIES OF FATE WHEN YOU MADE YOUR APPEARANCE IN THE CONSPIRACY OF THE XX AND WE TOOK A CLOSER LOOK AT YOU...

SEARCHING THROUGH YOUR PAST, WE DISCOVERED THAT ONE OF YOUR ANCESTORS HAD HAD A SHORT-LIVED AFFAIR WITH JAMES DUNCAN IN GALWAY. SHE'D BECOME PREGNANT NOT LONG BEFORE HIS DEATH. PERHAPS HE HAD GIVEN HER THE DOCUMENTS BEFORE PASSING?

HER NAME WAS MARY O'KEEFE, MR MCLANE. AND SHE NAMED HER SON ... HENRY. WHO, IN 1869, EMIGRATED WITH HIS YOUNG WIFE DORIS TO THE USA, WHERE THEY SETTLED DOWN IN BROOKLYN. I BELIEVE YOU KNOW THE REST.

HENRY ... O'KEEFE!

...OF WHOM YOU ARE THE LAST DESCENDANT. THEREFORE, THE HEIR TO THE ADVENTURERS' BRANCH OF THE *MAYFLOWER!* THEREFORE, THE MAN WHO HAS BEEN ENTRUSTED WITH THE LOCATION OF THE MOST CLOSELY GUARDED AMERICAN DOCUMENTS OF THE PAST FOUR CENTURIES: THE ORIGINAL MAYFLOWER COMPACT AND THE PURITANS' ACT OF RENUNCIATION!

AS THE CURRENT GODMOTHER OF THE PURITANS, I'VE VOWED TO DEDICATE MY LIFE TO THE RESTORATION OF OUR RIGHTS BY ANY MEANS NECESSARY. IF YOUR MEMORIES ALLOW US TO RECOVER THOSE DOCUMENTS, YOU HAVE MY WORD THAT YOU WILL BE FREE ONCE AND FOR ALL.

LET'S ASSUME THAT YOUR STORY IS TRUE AND THAT I'M WILLING TO GIVE YOU YOUR DAMNED PAPERS TO CLEAR MY SLATE. HOW AM I SUPPOSED TO FIND THEM?

WE'VE HAD TIME TO THINK ABOUT IT. OUR DOCTORS ARE JUST AS SKILLED AS PROFESSOR DOUGLAS IN AUGUSTA...

UNDER DEAR SUZANNE'S SUPERVISION, WE'RE GOING TO PREPARE YOU, AND THEN WE CAN ALL EXPLORE YOUR SUBCONSCIOUS TOGETHER.

15

17

OFFICER QUINCANNON TO CENTRAL! THAT PORSCHE WE GOT A CODE 22 ON ... JUST FLEW BY ME! IT'S HEADING DOWNTOWN ON OLYMPIC BOULEVARD. I'M IN PURSUIT.

POWAAA AAH

VROOOOO

...ALL YOU NEED IS LOVE... ALL YOU NEED IS LOVE, LOVE ...

LOVE IS ALL YOU N...

BETTY, YOU'RE AN IDIOT, GIRL...

CLICK

18

WELL, MA'AM? DID YOU THINK YOU WERE IN A VIDEO GAME OR SOMETHING?

OH, OFFICER, DON'T TELL ME YOU HAVEN'T TRIED *TARGA CHALLENGE III* YET! TO MOVE ON TO LEVEL 5, YOU HAVE TO...

...GET RID OF A MOTORCYCLE COP. SO SORRY. BYE-BYE!

VROOM

THAT B....

POOWAAAAAA

VROOM

19

YOU MUST BE JASON'S FRIEND? I WAS JUST CLOSING.

A HIGHWAY PATROL OFFICER ALMOST MADE ME LATE. SPEAKING OF WHICH, IF WE COULD TAKE YOUR CAR TO GO SOMEWHERE OUT OF THE WAY...

THAT SETTLES IT. YOU'RE DEFINITELY A FRIEND OF JASON'S.

HEY, MISS JUDITH! STILL SELLING WELL, THAT HOMY... HOMEOPA...?

HO-ME-O-PA-THY, MIKE! AND IT SELLS LIKE HOTCAKES!

IS IT SOME KIND OF SPECIALISED PHARMACY?

CALIFORNIANS ABSOLUTELY LOVE THIS SORT OF CONCEPT...

I'D HEARD ABOUT THIS ... KIND OF BAR BEFORE, BUT I'D NEVER...

THIS, TOO, IS SANTA MONICA, MISS BARNOWSKY. IN HERE, AT LEAST, WE'RE NOT CONSTANTLY BOTHERED BY LETCHES ON THE PROWL. ANYWAY, WHAT DID YOU WANT TO KNOW?

THE ONLY REDHEAD I'VE SEEN TONIGHT WAS THE ONE WITH OUR PHARMACIST. IT'S THURSDAY NIGHT. MAYBE THEY WENT TO ENJOY THE HAPPY HOUR AT THE NO MEN, NO BRA...

DAVID KNOWS ME WELL... I DID HAVE A FLING WITH EARL THORNTON. THAT BUS DRIVER WAS QUITE THE HUNK. BACK THEN HE LIVED IN A CABIN AT THE END OF ... PEARL AVENUE. THE WORST STREET IN NORTH GREEN FALLS.

IT WAS AFTER DWIGHT RIGBY, DAVID'S FATHER, RAPED ME. FOLLOWING THAT ... EXPERIENCE, I ATTEMPTED TO REVERSE THE DIRECTION OF DOMINATION, SO TO SPEAK...

...AND I TRIED TO TAKE JUST ABOUT EVERY PRETTY BOY IN THAT DUMP FOR A TEST DRIVE. I STILL DON'T UNDERSTAND WHY, BUT I HAD A SORT OF ONE-NIGHT-STAND OVERDOSE AFTER JASON MCLANE BLEW THROUGH TOWN. SO I LEFT...

I THINK WE'RE GOING TO HAVE TO CUT THE GIRL TALK SHORT...

FOLLOW ME.

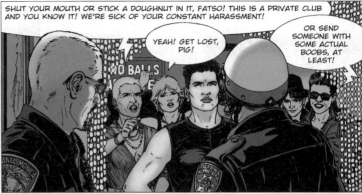

SHUT YOUR MOUTH OR STICK A DOUGHNUT IN IT, FATSO! THIS IS A PRIVATE CLUB AND YOU KNOW IT! WE'RE SICK OF YOUR CONSTANT HARASSMENT!

YEAH! GET LOST, PIG!

OR SEND SOMEONE WITH SOME ACTUAL BOOBS, AT LEAST!

I'M WARNING YOU! IF YOU ATTEMPT TO OBSTRUCT...

HOW DO YOU PLAN ON GETTING TO GREEN FALLS, HONEY? IT'S PRETTY FAR...

I IMAGINE THE FASTEST WAY WOULD BE TO FLY TO DENVER, THEN TAKE A BUS.

SINCE MONEY SEEMS TO BE NO OBJECT, TAKE THIS CAB DIRECTLY TO CAMARILLO AIRPORT. ASK FOR RODRIGO. HANDSOME AND EFFICIENT...

IT'S BEEN A PLEASURE CROSSING PATHS WITH YOU, BETTY. WHEN YOU SEE OUR NUMBER XIII, COULD YOU GIVE HIM A LITTLE PRESENT FROM ME?

OF COURSE. IF YOU HAVE IT WITH YOU, GIVE IT TO ME.

WHAT?!... WHAT A BUNCH OF... OH? WHERE?... OK. THANKS, DOLL.

SPECIAL AGENTS DODSON AND BLOOM? I'M DETECTIVE DICKINSON, AND THIS IS AGENT QUINCANNON. WE ARE REALLY SORRY TO INFORM YOU THAT...

...YOU COULDN'T MANAGE TO ARREST SUSPECT BETTY BARNOWSKY, I KNOW. I'VE JUST BEEN TOLD THAT SHE USED HER CREDIT CARD TO PAY FOR A PRIVATE FLIGHT TO DENVER.

SORRY WE GOTTA LEAVE ALREADY. WE CAN GO FOR DRINKS ANOTHER TIME, OK?

...AND LEAN ON THE AIRPORT POLICE. I WANT THEM TO GRAB HER THE MOMENT SHE LANDS IN DENVER! NOBODY GETS OFF THE PLANE BEFORE WE ARRIVE.

TELL ME, RODRIGO, WOULD YOU MIND DROPPING ME OFF ON A ROAD NEAR GREEN FALLS?

I'VE LOCATED A NICE, STRAIGHT STRETCH IN THE BOONIES THAT SHOULDN'T BE VERY BUSY.

THANKS, RODRIGO. I HOPE I WON'T BE CAUSING YOU TOO MUCH TROUBLE.

TROUBLE? THE OFFICIAL VERSION WILL SAY THAT I HAD TO TOUCH DOWN BECAUSE OF ENGINE PROBLEMS, AND IT SCARED YOU OFF GETTING BACK ON BOARD... ADIOS, BONITA PELIRROJA!*

REMARKABLY BUSY ROADS IN YOUR COUNTY, SHERIFF!

WHAT... WHAT ARE YOU DOING HERE? WHO ARE YOU?

HI, I'M BETTY BARNOWSKY! A TRUCKER DROPPED ME OFF ABOUT A MILE FROM HERE. I'M ON MY WAY TO GREEN FALLS TO SEE AN OLD FRIEND, EARL THORNTON. IT'D BE REAL SWEET OF YOU TO DRIVE ME TO TOWN — I'M EXHAUSTED...

*GOODBYE, BEAUTIFUL REDHEAD...

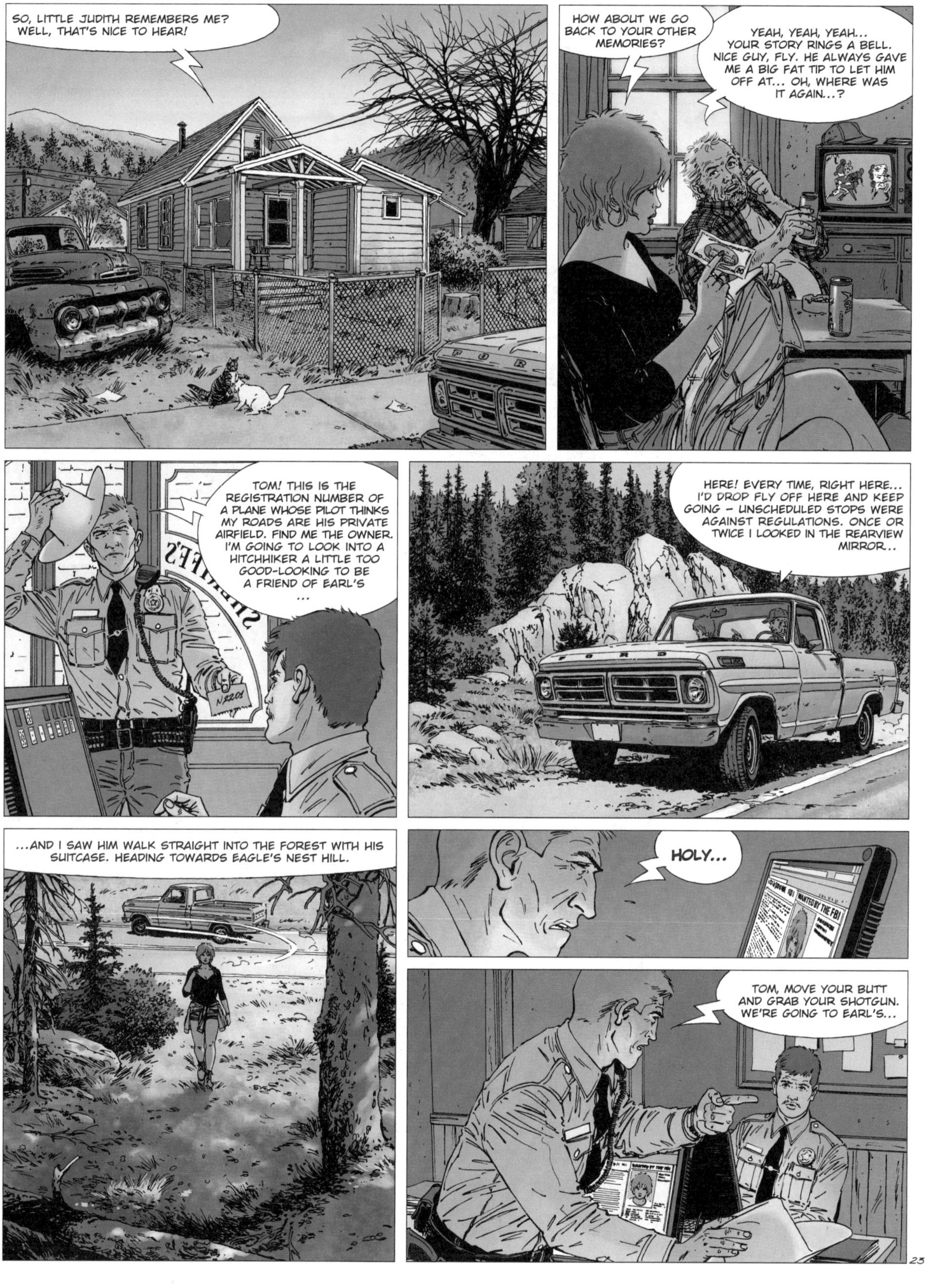
SO, LITTLE JUDITH REMEMBERS ME? WELL, THAT'S NICE TO HEAR!
HOW ABOUT WE GO BACK TO YOUR OTHER MEMORIES?
YEAH, YEAH, YEAH... YOUR STORY RINGS A BELL. NICE GUY, FLY. HE ALWAYS GAVE ME A BIG FAT TIP TO LET HIM OFF AT... OH, WHERE WAS IT AGAIN...?
TOM! THIS IS THE REGISTRATION NUMBER OF A PLANE WHOSE PILOT THINKS MY ROADS ARE HIS PRIVATE AIRFIELD. FIND ME THE OWNER. I'M GOING TO LOOK INTO A HITCHHIKER A LITTLE TOO GOOD-LOOKING TO BE A FRIEND OF EARL'S ...
HERE! EVERY TIME, RIGHT HERE... I'D DROP FLY OFF HERE AND KEEP GOING – UNSCHEDULED STOPS WERE AGAINST REGULATIONS. ONCE OR TWICE I LOOKED IN THE REARVIEW MIRROR...
FORD
...AND I SAW HIM WALK STRAIGHT INTO THE FOREST WITH HIS SUITCASE. HEADING TOWARDS EAGLE'S NEST HILL.
HOLY...
WANTED BY THE FBI
TOM, MOVE YOUR BUTT AND GRAB YOUR SHOTGUN. WE'RE GOING TO EARL'S...
23

HELLO, MR MCLANE. IT'S TIME TO GO.

ACTUALLY, I THINK IT'S TIME FOR YOU TO TELL ME WHAT YOU'RE DOING HERE, DOCTOR. I DON'T GET IT. I PICKED YOUR NAME AT RANDOM FROM THE AUGUSTA PHONE BOOK*...

AN UNFORTUNATE COINCIDENCE. I SWEAR TO YOU I HAD NO IDEA MY FATHER WORKED FOR ... THESE PEOPLE. HE CALLED ME LAST WEEK, FRANTIC. TOLD ME THAT HE KNEW YOU WERE MY PATIENT, AND THAT IF I WANTED HIM TO LIVE, I HAD TO COOPERA...

SUZANNE! HERE ALREADY?

WE... WE WERE WAITING FOR YOU.

LET'S HUSTLE, THEN! I CAN'T WAIT TO HEAR YOU TELL US ALL THE SECRETS BURIED IN YOUR BRAIN, NUMBER XIII!

DON'T WORRY. I MADE SURE THE SAFETY PROTOCOLS FROM AUGUSTA WERE STRICTLY FOLLOWED HERE AS WELL. EVERYTHING WILL BE FINE.

HOW AM I SUPPOSED TO ANSWER? 'I'M SO GLAD I MET YOU'?...

*SEE VOLUME 19: *THE DAY OF THE MAYFLOWER.*

THE ANAESTHETIC IS FADING. IT'S TIME FOR THE HYPNOSIS...

EVERYTHING SEEMS IN ORDER. PROCEED.

RELAX. LET YOUR MEMORIES FLOAT TO THE SURFACE... YOU'RE ABOUT 12. YOU'RE A GOOD STUDENT...

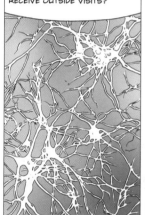

LIFE AT ST ANDREWS ORPHANAGE IN DENVER CENTRES AROUND THE SCHOOL YEAR... DO YOU EVER RECEIVE OUTSIDE VISITS?

VISITS?... YES. IT'S THANKSGIVING. MY GOD-FATHER HAS COME TO GET ME, LIKE EVERY YEAR.

WE'RE GOING BACK TO GREEN FALLS...

WE'RE NOT GOING TO SEE ZEKE, WHICH MAKES ME A LITTLE SAD... WE'RE GOING STRAIGHT TO THE CABIN.

I'M STILL HAPPY, BECAUSE I KNOW I'M GOING TO SEE...

PRIVATE PROPERTY NO TRESPASSING

THREE SPRINGS!

CRACK

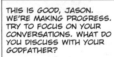

THIS IS GOOD, JASON. WE'RE MAKING PROGRESS. TRY TO FOCUS ON YOUR CONVERSATIONS. WHAT DO YOU DISCUSS WITH YOUR GODFATHER?

HE EXPLAINS THAT IT'S IMPORTANT FOR ME TO CONTINUE MY HISTORY AND LANGUAGE LESSONS. THAT I MUST BECOME EDUCATED BECAUSE HEAVY RESPONSIBILITIES AWAIT ME.

ONE DAY, HE SAID, I'D BECOME...

...THE CUSTODIAN OF AN IMPORTANT MORAL AND FINANCIAL HERITAGE DATING BACK TO THE ORIGINS OF AMERICA.

THAT HERITAGE IS RECORDED IN DOCUMENTS, JASON. ARE THEY IN THE CABIN?

DOCUMENTS?... YES. ONE DAY, MY GODFATHER SHOWED ME SOME VERY OLD PAPERS. HE SAID...

WHEN YOU TURN 21, THESE DOCUMENTS WILL BECOME YOUR RESPONSIBILITY ALONE.

NOW YOU MUST SWEAR TO PROTECT THEM, ALWAYS, UNTIL THE DAY YOU USE THEM OR THE DAY YOU PASS THEM ON TO YOUR OWN HEIR.

BUT... I DON'T UNDERSTAND WHAT...

SOMEDAY YOU WILL, JASON, I PROMISE. IN THE MEANTIME, TRUST ME ... AND SWEAR!

I SWEAR!

AND IF THE HEIR EVER LOSES HIS WAY... ALWAYS FOLLOW THE WAMPANOAG ARROW.

27

KEEP PUSHING, SUZANNE. WE MUST FIND OUT WHERE THOSE DOCUMENTS ARE HIDDEN.

RELAX, JASON. FOCUS ON A SINGLE QUESTION: WHERE ARE THE DOCUMENTS? WHAT HAPPENED WHEN YOU WERE 21?

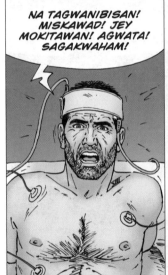

NA TAGWANIBISAN! MISKAWAD! JEY MOKITAWAN! AGWATA! SAGAKWAHAM!

WHAT WAS THAT? IT'S COMPLETE GIBBERISH! SUZANNE?

MADAM, HE'S EXHAUSTED. I RECOMMEND WE INTERRUPT THE...

OUT OF THE QUESTION! DR LEVINSON, SEND ANOTHER STIMULUS. HE MUST TALK. AND I'M WARNING YOU: IN AN INTELLIGIBLE LANGUAGE THIS TIME!

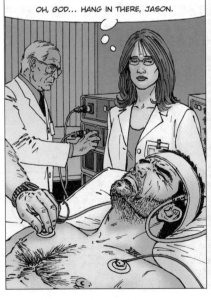

OH, GOD... HANG IN THERE, JASON.

30

ONE LAST EFFORT, JASON. TRY TO REMEMBER, I BEG YOU...

YES... I... I SEE... SCHOOL IS BACK IN SESSION TOMORROW.

MY GODFATHER TAKES ME BACK TO THE ORPHANAGE...

St ANDREWS ORPHANAGE

TAXI

IT WAS ALWAYS GREAT TO SEE JIM AND MIKE AGAIN. I WAS THE ONLY ONE WHO EVER TRAVELLED OUTSIDE ST ANDREWS, SO THEY WANTED ME TO TELL THEM EVERYTHING.

I KNEW WHAT I COULD MENTION ABOUT MY STAYS AT THE CABIN. THE REST HAD TO REMAIN SECRET. MY FRIENDS WERE QUITE IMPRESSED WITH THE FEW WORDS I'D LEARNED IN A NATIVE AMERICAN LANGUAGE...

I HAD TO START ALL OVER IN THE EVENING, AND THEY DEMANDED EVEN MORE DETAILS! THIS TIME I...

EENY, MEENY, MINY ... MO! KEAN, GET UP AND COME WITH ME.

NO! LEAVE HIM ALONE!

LEAVE HIM!

29

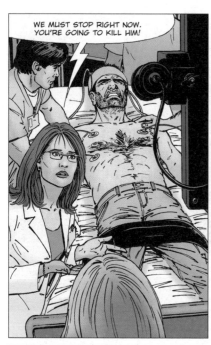

WE MUST STOP RIGHT NOW. YOU'RE GOING TO KILL HIM!

WHAT WAS THAT STRANGE LANGUAGE HE USED BEFORE REMEMBERING HIS DORMITORY STORIES?

WE'LL CHECK WITH OUR SPECIALISTS, MADAM. PERHAPS IT WAS THAT NATIVE AMERICAN LANGUAGE HE MENTIONED?

THE HEIRS OF THE THIRD BRANCH WERE REALLY CLEVER. IF THEY'RE USING AN UNKNOWN LANGUAGE TO PASS ON THEIR SECRETS...

I'M AFRAID WE'RE AT AN IMPASSE. IF OUR MAN IS AMNESIC, THERE'S EVERY CHANCE HE WON'T EVEN BE ABLE TO TRANSLATE HIS OWN WORDS.

GO TO DENVER WITH MCLANE. IF SOMEONE HAD PERMISSION TO TAKE THE BOY OUT OF THE ORPHANAGE, THEN THERE HAS TO BE A RECORD OF HIS IDENTITY.

LOOK INTO IT. TRACK DOWN THE THIRD BRANCH GODFATHER ... AND HOPEFULLY MCLANE WILL RECOVER **ALL** HIS MEMORIES.

HANDS UP! DON'T MOVE!

TONK

CRRACK

BANG

TOM!... GET HER!

DENVER AIR TRAFFIC CONTROL...

WHAT DO YOU MEAN, HE DECIDED TO TURN AROUND?

LIKE IT'S WRITTEN: SHORTLY BEFORE REACHING DENVER, THE PILOT REPORTED ENGINE PROBLEMS OVER THE RADIO, THEN TURNED BACK TOWARDS CAMARILLO.

SO. WHAT DO WE DO?

WE WAIT. THAT EMERGENCY LANDING IS SUSPICIOUS. GET OUR GUYS AT CAMARILLO AIRPORT ON THE HORN. HAVE THEM CALL US AS SOON AS THEY HAVE THE PILOT.

I'VE ALREADY BEEN THERE, YOU KNOW. ST ANDREWS ORPHANAGE WAS REPLACED BY A SHOPPING MALL. YOU WON'T FIND ANYTHING THERE*.

SO YOU WEREN'T TOLD THAT THE CHILDREN WERE RELOCATED ABOUT 30 MILES FROM THE ORIGINAL SITE? APPARENTLY, THE ARCHIVES WENT WITH THEM.

DENVER, MA'AM. WE'RE STARTING OUR APPROACH.

*SEE VOLUME 6: THE JASON FLY CASE.

31

33

...OF COURSE, MR FLY. FORMER RESIDENTS RETAIN PERMANENT ACCESS TO THEIR FILE. GIVE ME A SECOND... AH! HERE IT IS.

THE RELEASE FORM SIGNED BY YOUR FATHER IS QUITE CLEAR. THE ONLY PERSON AUTHORISED TO TAKE RESPONSIBILITY FOR YOU – ASIDE FROM THE AUTHORITIES – WAS A BART DORMANN... LISTED AS RESIDING IN EAGLE'S NEST HILL WHEN IN THE UNITED STATES – A PLACE LOCATED RIGHT NEXT TO ... THE TOWN OF GREEN FALLS, COLORADO.

AND WHEN NOT *IN THE UNITED STATES*, WHERE COULD HE BE CONTACTED?

ONE MOMENT... AH! THERE'S A POSTAL BOX NUMBER IN LEIDEN... THE NETHERLANDS. IT'S NUMBER 2112...

SEE? IT WAS TOTALLY WORTH COMING! ACCORDING TO YOUR FILE, YOU KNOW GREEN FALLS WELL, DON'T YOU? ALL YOU HAVE TO DO IS GUIDE US, THEN.

SPECIAL AGENT DODSON? WE HAVE THE PILOT. HE HAD TO STOP IN BOULDER TO REFUEL. HE SAYS HIS PAS-SENGER REFUSED TO GET BACK ON THE PLANE AFTER THE BREAKDOWN... THAT'S RIGHT. NEAR GREEN FALLS... THE LOCAL SHERIFF ALSO PLACED A REQUEST FOR IDENTIFICATION OF THE PILOT...

TOM, WHY DON'T YOU GO WASH THE CAR INSTEAD OF SCREWING AROUND? IT'S FILTHY.

DRIIING DRIIING

SHERIFF REISMAN? DODSON, FBI. YOU'RE THE ONE WHO SAW THAT PRIVATE PLANE LAND?... WERE YOU ABLE TO SEE IF THERE WAS A REDHEADED WOMAN INSIDE?

INSIDE, NOPE. BUT I DID PICK UP THAT REDHEAD OF YOURS ON THE ROAD. I WAS ABOUT TO CALL YOU WITH A SURPRISE: WE'VE PUT HER ON ICE FOR YOU, BOYS!

32

GREEN FALLS, AN HOUR AND TWELVE MINUTES LATER...

IT'S BEST TO KEEP A LOW PROFILE AROUND HERE. TRUST ME ON THIS. WAIT HERE; THIS SHOULD ONLY TAKE A FEW MINUTES.

HEY, HEY, HEY... LOOKIT WHO'S DROPPED BY TO SAY HELLO*! IF IT AIN'T THE FAMOUS NUMBER XIII!

THE NEWS SAID YOU WERE WANTED FOR BLOWING UP A PRISON... YOU'VE MOVED UP SINCE THE SEAVIEW, BUDDY! AND THERE'S A JUICY REWARD FOR YOUR CAPTURE! MAGGIE, CALL THE SHERIFF. WE'RE GONNA HAVE A WORD WITH MR TROUBLE HERE...

KEEP A LOW PROFILE, HUH? IS HE TRYING TO GET ARRESTED?

FBI! EVERYBODY FREEZE!

*SEE VOLUME 7: *THE NIGHT OF AUGUST THIRD.*

33

35

THIS MAN IS OURS. UNLESS YOU WANT TO GET SLAPPED WITH OBSTRUCTING AN FBI INVESTIGATION...

WELL, DANG! YOU GOT HERE FAST...

EVERY TIME THAT GUY SHOWS UP HERE, HE STARTS A RIOT. DO ME A FAVOUR: GRAB YOUR PACKAGE AND GET OUT OF THIS COUNTY ON THE DOUBLE.

OUR ... PACKAGE?

LIKE I TOLD YOUR COLLEAGUE, THE CHICK'S WAITING FOR YOU IN HER CELL. FOLLOW MY CRUISER TO THE OFFICE – THEN GOOD RIDDANCE!

RELAX, DODSON. I DON'T WANT YOU TO FALL ASLEEP AT THE WHEEL. IF YOU WANT THE KEYS BACK, YOU'RE GOING TO HAVE TO FINISH THIS BURGER AND TAKE A NAP IN THE CAR.

ANYWAY, THE SHERIFF TOLD US SHE WAS IN A CELL, AND I DON'T SEE HOW...

THE STUPIDITY OF COUNTRY COPS IN THIS LAND OF OURS KNOWS NO BOUNDS. HAVE YOU FORGOTTEN THE PLYMOUTH PD*?

BETTY?!

HERE! I'LL EVEN THROW IN THE HANDCUFFS. SOUVENIR OF GREEN FALLS – PROVIDED YOU RID US OF THESE PARASITES!

JASON?! BUT ... WHAT ARE YOU DOING HERE? WHAT ABOUT JONES? CARRINGTON?

THEY'RE FINE. I THINK...

SEEING THAT YOU TWO KNOW EACH OTHER, I'D LIKE TO KNOW WHAT YOU ARE DOING HERE, MY DEAR. SPEAK FREELY. WE'RE VERY GOOD FRIENDS OF MR MCLANE'S...

*SEE VOLUME 20: THE BAIT.

34

THANK YOU FOR THIS RECAP OF YOUR EXCITING ADVENTURES, MS BARNOWSKY. I SEE THAT NUMBER XIII CAN COUNT ON ALL OF HIS FRIENDS.

I'LL BE KEEPING MR HATTAWAY'S MEMOIRS, IF YOU DON'T MIND. MOREOVER, I'D LIKE TO KNOW WHAT YOU FOUND IN THAT CABIN BEFORE THAT IDIOT SHERIFF INTERRUPTED YOU.

JASON? SHOULD I...?

GO AHEAD, BETTY. UNLESS WE COLLABORATE, THESE MANIACS WILL TAKE IT OUT ON INNOCENT PEOPLE. THEY MADE THAT CLEAR TO CARRINGTON, JONES AND ME.

ALL RIGHT... WELL, ACTUALLY, THERE WAS NOTHING EXCEPT A POSTER ADVERTISING THE CHARMS OF LAKE CHAMPLAIN IN VERMONT. A NATIVE AMERICAN ARROW WAS STUCK INTO THE MAP NEAR THE TOWN OF SHELBURNE. I PUT THE POSTER IN MY JACKET POCKET, BUT I MUST HAVE LOST IT IN THE SHERIFF'S CRUISER ...

DO YOU REMEMBER, MCLANE? DURING HYPNOSIS, YOU QUOTED THAT INDIAN WHO WAS IN THE CABIN WITH YOUR GODFATHER: 'AND IF THE HEIR EVER LOSES HIS WAY... ALWAYS FOLLOW THE WAMPANOAG ARROW.'

BACK TO DENVER, IKE! IN THE MEANTIME, I'LL LOOK FOR THE AIRPORT CLOSEST TO SHELBURNE.

VVRROOO

SO, IS THAT CAR CLEAN AT LAST?

LIKE NEW! BY THE WAY, I FOUND THIS OLD AD ON THE BACKSEAT. IS IT YOURS, OR SHOULD I CHUCK IT?

LAKE CHAMPLAIN REGION

BURLINGTON INTERNATIONAL AIRPORT, VERMONT, SIX MILES FROM SHELBURNE...

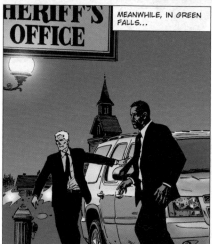

MEANWHILE, IN GREEN FALLS...

FBI! WHERE'S THE PRISONER?

THE PRISONER?! BUT ... YOUR COLLEAGUES ALREADY PICKED HER UP.

STOP HERE, BUCK. AND REMEMBER, EVERYONE: WE'RE TWO TOURIST COUPLES HERE TO PAY A VISIT TO THE 'LAKE MONSTER'.

THAT'S ALL YOU'VE GOT?

AN OLD AD THAT MUST HAVE FALLEN OUT OF HER POCKET IN THE CAR. SHE TOOK THE REST OF HER STUFF WITH HER. IT'S NOT LIKE I COULD HAVE KNOWN...

NOTHING IN THE CELL, MEL.

SHELBURNE, ON LAKE CHAMPLAIN... SLIM, BUT ... THAT'S ALL WE'VE GOT. OK! BACK TO DENVER, AND WE'LL TAKE THE JET TO BURLINGTON.

36

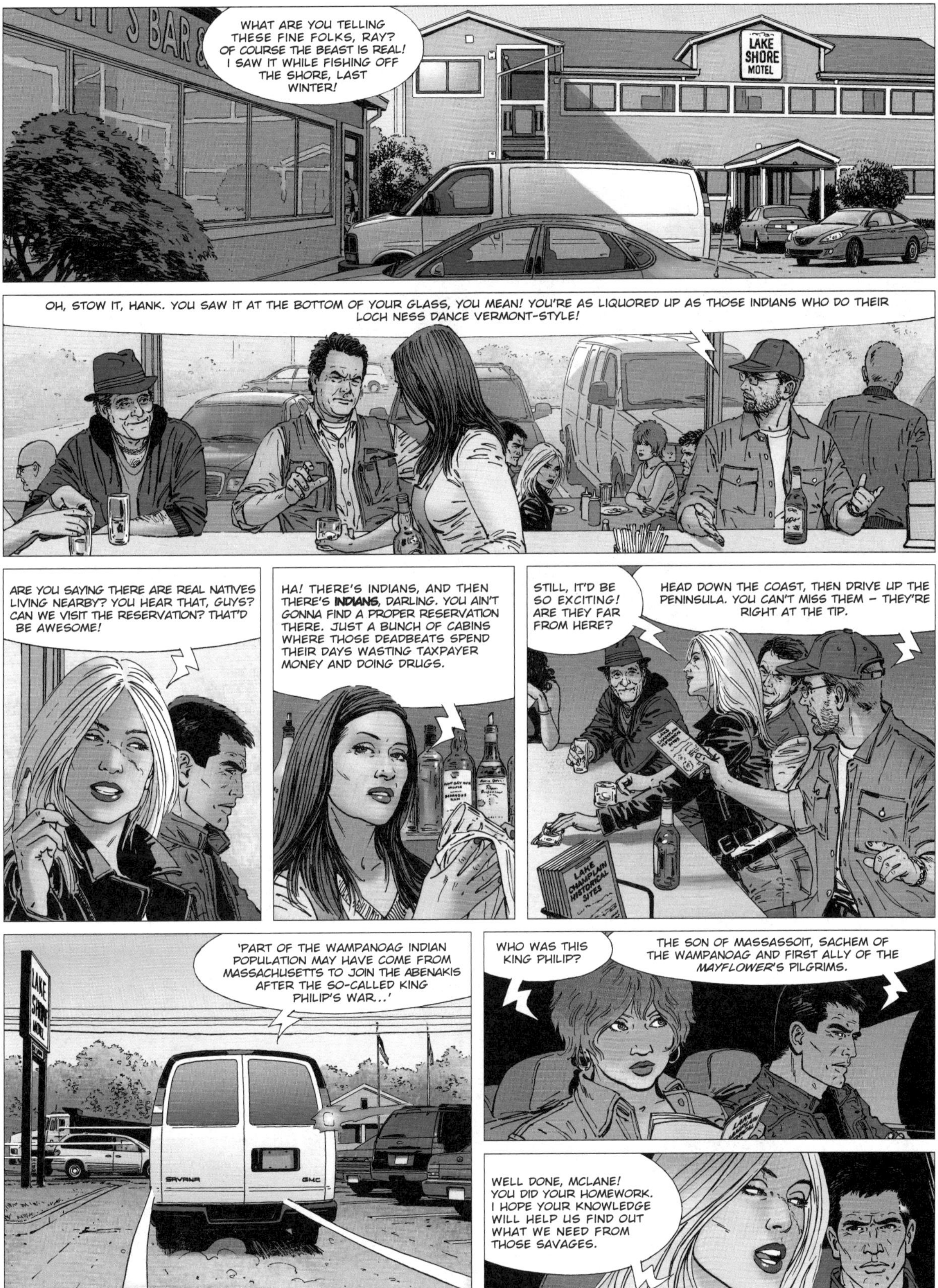
WHAT ARE YOU TELLING THESE FINE FOLKS, RAY? OF COURSE THE BEAST IS REAL! I SAW IT WHILE FISHING OFF THE SHORE, LAST WINTER!
LAKE SHORE MOTEL
OH, STOW IT, HANK. YOU SAW IT AT THE BOTTOM OF YOUR GLASS, YOU MEAN! YOU'RE AS LIQUORED UP AS THOSE INDIANS WHO DO THEIR LOCH NESS DANCE VERMONT-STYLE!
ARE YOU SAYING THERE ARE REAL NATIVES LIVING NEARBY? YOU HEAR THAT, GUYS? CAN WE VISIT THE RESERVATION? THAT'D BE AWESOME!
HA! THERE'S INDIANS, AND THEN THERE'S **INDIANS**, DARLING. YOU AIN'T GONNA FIND A PROPER RESERVATION THERE. JUST A BUNCH OF CABINS WHERE THOSE DEADBEATS SPEND THEIR DAYS WASTING TAXPAYER MONEY AND DOING DRUGS.
STILL, IT'D BE SO EXCITING! ARE THEY FAR FROM HERE?
HEAD DOWN THE COAST, THEN DRIVE UP THE PENINSULA. YOU CAN'T MISS THEM – THEY'RE RIGHT AT THE TIP.
LAKE CHAMPLAIN HISTORICAL SITES
'PART OF THE WAMPANOAG INDIAN POPULATION MAY HAVE COME FROM MASSACHUSETTS TO JOIN THE ABENAKIS AFTER THE SO-CALLED KING PHILIP'S WAR...'
WHO WAS THIS KING PHILIP?
THE SON OF MASSASSOIT, SACHEM OF THE WAMPANOAG AND FIRST ALLY OF THE *MAYFLOWER*'S PILGRIMS.
WELL DONE, MCLANE! YOU DID YOUR HOMEWORK. I HOPE YOUR KNOWLEDGE WILL HELP US FIND OUT WHAT WE NEED FROM THOSE SAVAGES.
37

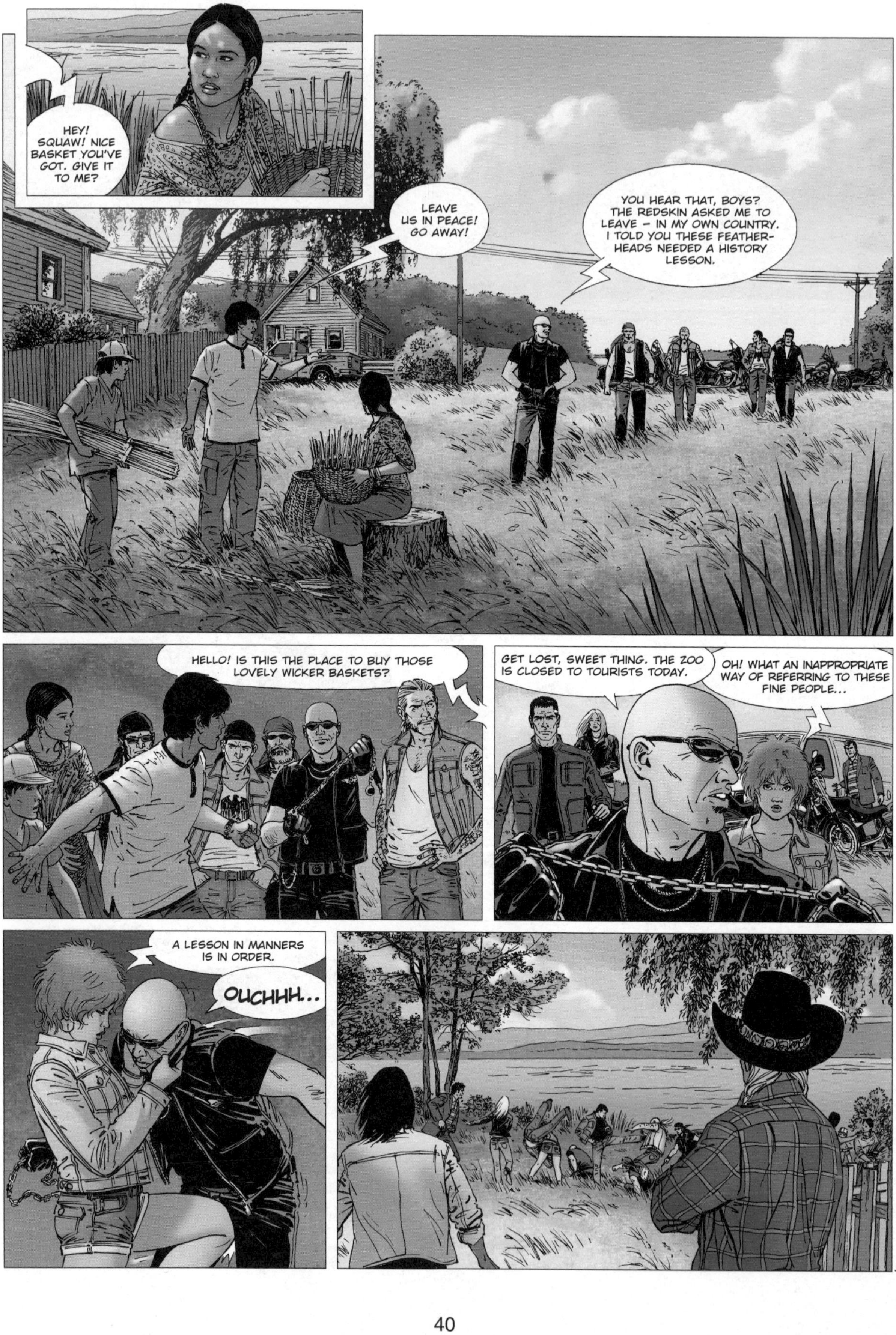

HEY! SQUAW! NICE BASKET YOU'VE GOT. GIVE IT TO ME?
LEAVE US IN PEACE! GO AWAY!
YOU HEAR THAT, BOYS? THE REDSKIN ASKED ME TO LEAVE – IN MY OWN COUNTRY. I TOLD YOU THESE FEATHER-HEADS NEEDED A HISTORY LESSON.
HELLO! IS THIS THE PLACE TO BUY THOSE LOVELY WICKER BASKETS?
GET LOST, SWEET THING. THE ZOO IS CLOSED TO TOURISTS TODAY.
OH! WHAT AN INAPPROPRIATE WAY OF REFERRING TO THESE FINE PEOPLE...
A LESSON IN MANNERS IS IN ORDER.
OUCHHH...
38

EASY, BETTY! THEY'VE HAD ENOUGH.

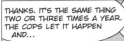

THANKS. IT'S THE SAME THING TWO OR THREE TIMES A YEAR. THE COPS LET IT HAPPEN AND...

OK, OK... WE'RE NOT HERE TO MEDDLE IN INDIAN POLITICS. WE'RE LOOKING FOR ONE OF YOU WHO LIVED IN COLORADO NEAR GREEN FALLS ABOUT 30 YEARS AGO.

HEY! I'M TALKING TO YOU! DID YOU UNDERSTAND THE QUESTION?

GREAT DIPLOMACY, THERE... THEY MUST THINK WE'RE COPS NOW. LET'S GO. WE'LL HAVE TO FIND A WAY TO REGAIN THEIR TRUST LATER.

I HAVE TO SLIP AWAY TONIGHT WITHOUT OUR KEEPERS KNOWING. DO YOU REMEMBER THAT SPADS TRICK? EXACTLY TWO HOURS AFTER SUNDOWN, TAKE CARE OF YOUR THUG. I'LL HANDLE JULIANNE, AND WE'LL MEET IN THE HALLWAY.

39

NO SNORING – AND DON'T TRY TO PLAY THE 'ROVING HANDS' GAME. THIS FAKE-COUPLE ROUTINE STOPS HERE. GET IT?

DON'T WORRY. I DON'T LIKE 'EM CHUBBY.

LAKE SHORE MOTEL

RRRHH... RRRHH...

HERE!...

FROM 'CHUBBY' WITH LOVE!

WHEN THAT OAF WAKES UP, HE'LL HAVE NO IDEA WHAT HAPPENED. WHAT'S THE PLAN?

JULIANNE IS OUT TOO. KEEP AN EYE ON THEM. IF THEY STIR, GIVE THEM ANOTHER 'SLEEPING PILL'. I SHOULD BE BACK BEFORE DAWN.

ONE LAST THING, JUST IN CASE... THE DOROTHY THAT JIM DRAKE MENTIONED – REMEMBER? IT WAS HIS CAT, THE ONE YOU SAVED FROM THE FIRE. THERE WAS A MEMORY CARD HIDDEN IN ITS COLLAR! I RECOVERED IT AND SENT IT TO ARMAND, JUST IN CASE. I ALSO PICKED UP THESE PICTURES AT DWIGHT RIGBY'S...

YOU ABSOLUTELY ROCK, DUCHESS!

COME SIT WITH ME, JASON. I'VE BEEN WAITING FOR YOU FOR SO LONG.

ARE YOU ... THREE SPRINGS? I THINK I SAW YOU IN...

...ONE OF YOUR MEMORIES? THIS AFTERNOON, I RECOGNISED YOUR EYES, SON. THEY TOLD ME YOU'VE FORGOTTEN YOUR PAST.

THAT'S THE THING. I NEED TO KNOW MORE ABOUT A MAN NAMED BART DORMANN AND ABOUT THE TWO GROUPS THAT WERE ON THE *MAYFLOWER*.

ONE THING AT A TIME.

FIRST, THOSE WHO TOLD YOU ABOUT **TWO** GROUPS DON'T KNOW THE TRUTH. UNLESS THEY LIED TO YOU DELIBERATELY. IN FACT, THERE WERE **THREE** GROUPS... AND THAT'S THE SOURCE OF THE TRAGEDY THAT'S BEEN PLAYING OUT FOR FOUR CENTURIES.

YOUR ADOPTIVE FATHER, JONATHAN, WAS THE LAST LEADER OF THE THIRD *MAYFLOWER* GROUP. HE'D CHOSEN BART, HIS FORMER CELL-MATE, TO BE YOUR 'GODFATHER'.

AFTER YOUR FATHER DIED, EVERY YEAR AT THANKSGIVING, BART AND I HAD YOU OVER TO START YOUR EDUCATION AS HEIR OF THE THIRD BRANCH ... UNTIL YOU VANISHED FROM BOULDER, SHORTLY AFTER GRADUATING.

BEFORE LEAVING THE COUNTRY TO GO HIDE THE THIRD BRANCH'S LEGACY, YOUR GODFATHER LEFT ME THIS, IN CASE YOU REAPPEARED. YOU DON'T REMEMBER, BUT THIS IS THE STORY OF YOUR ORIGINS. IT WILL HELP YOU UNDERSTAND WHERE YOU COME FROM.

SHA NAH HEH! SETT KUTT!

HEY?!

BLAM BLAM

SO, YOU RED TRASH! DID YOU THINK YOU COULD AMBUSH US LIKE THAT AND WE WOULDN'T COME BACK TO SETTLE IT?

COME OUT, COME OUT, WHEREVER YOU...

HRRR...

HEY, HANK, YOU OK, MAN?

HOLY SHIT! HANK!

YOU?! YOU'RE STILL HERE?... HEY... DON'T SCREW AROUND WITH THAT TOMAHAWK! I'VE GOT A GUN...

I STILL LIKE MY CHANCES.

BANG

44

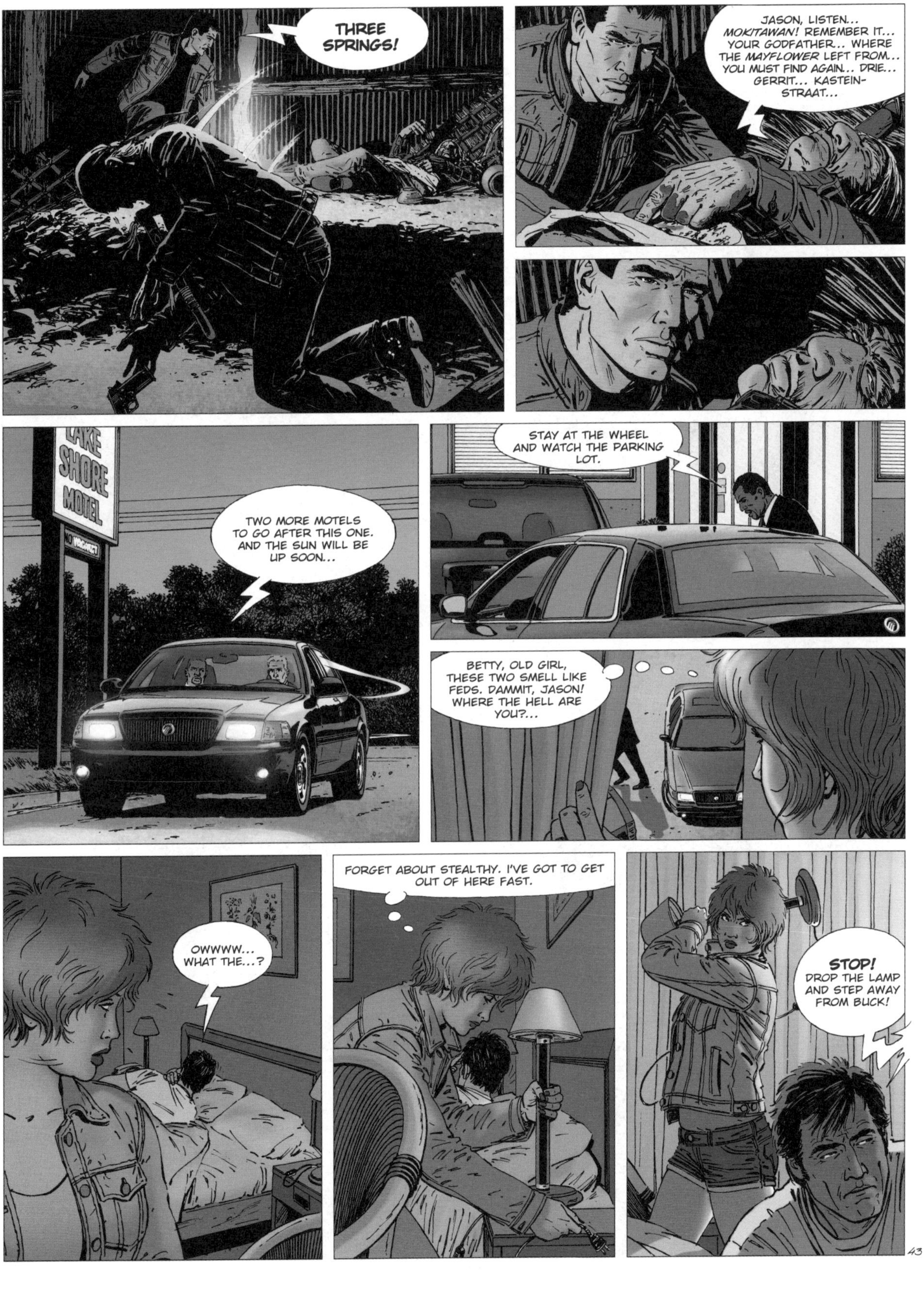
THREE SPRINGS!
JASON, LISTEN... MOKITAWAN! REMEMBER IT... YOUR GODFATHER... WHERE THE MAYFLOWER LEFT FROM... YOU MUST FIND AGAIN... DRIE... GERRIT... KASTEIN-STRAAT...
LAKE SHORE MOTEL
NO VACANCY
TWO MORE MOTELS TO GO AFTER THIS ONE. AND THE SUN WILL BE UP SOON...
STAY AT THE WHEEL AND WATCH THE PARKING LOT.
BETTY, OLD GIRL, THESE TWO SMELL LIKE FEDS. DAMMIT, JASON! WHERE THE HELL ARE YOU?...
OWWWW... WHAT THE...?
FORGET ABOUT STEALTHY. I'VE GOT TO GET OUT OF HERE FAST.
STOP! DROP THE LAMP AND STEP AWAY FROM BUCK!
43

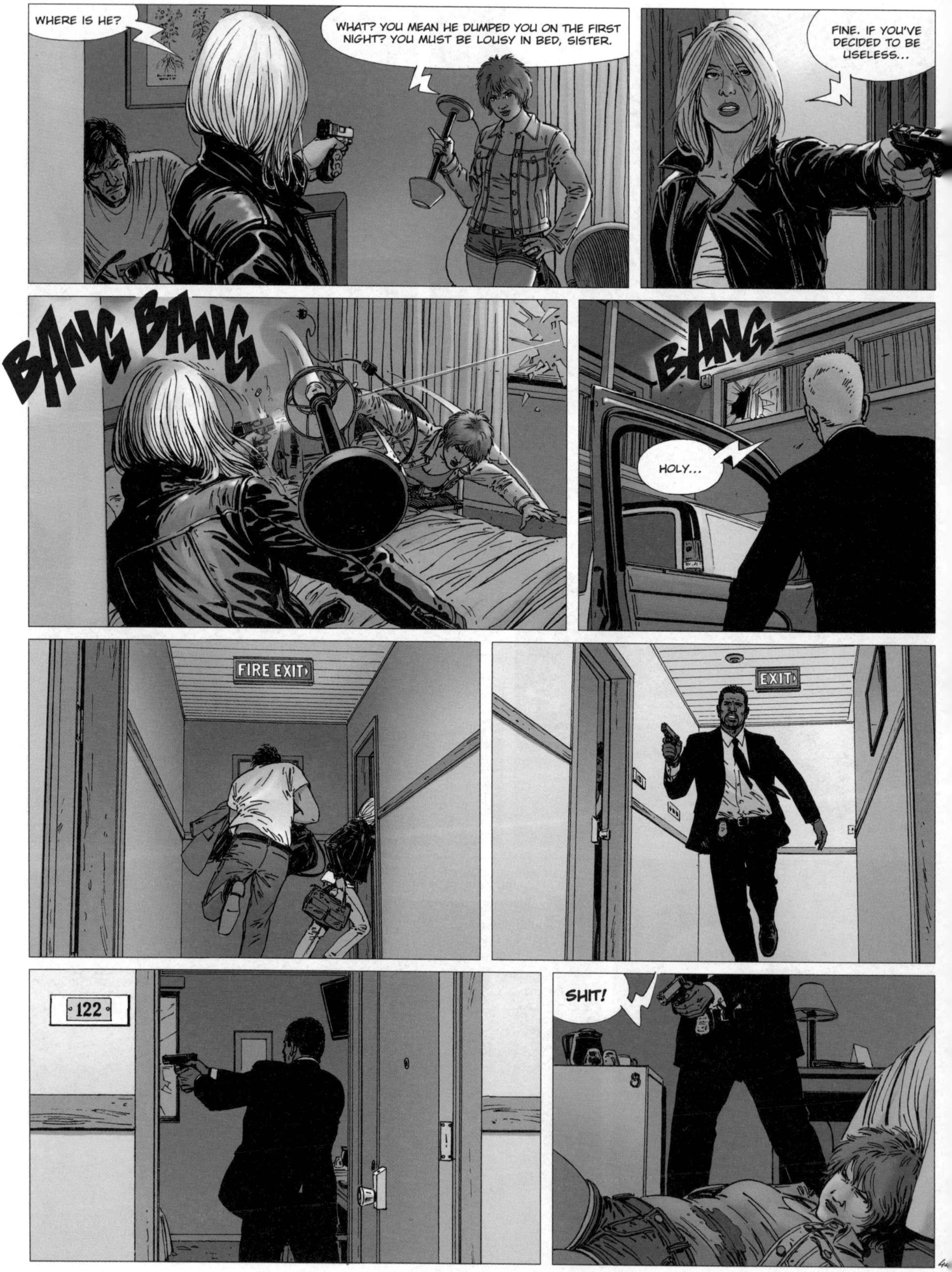
WHERE IS HE?
WHAT? YOU MEAN HE DUMPED YOU ON THE FIRST NIGHT? YOU MUST BE LOUSY IN BED, SISTER.
FINE. IF YOU'VE DECIDED TO BE USELESS...
BANG BANG
BANG
HOLY...
FIRE EXIT
EXIT
122
SHIT!

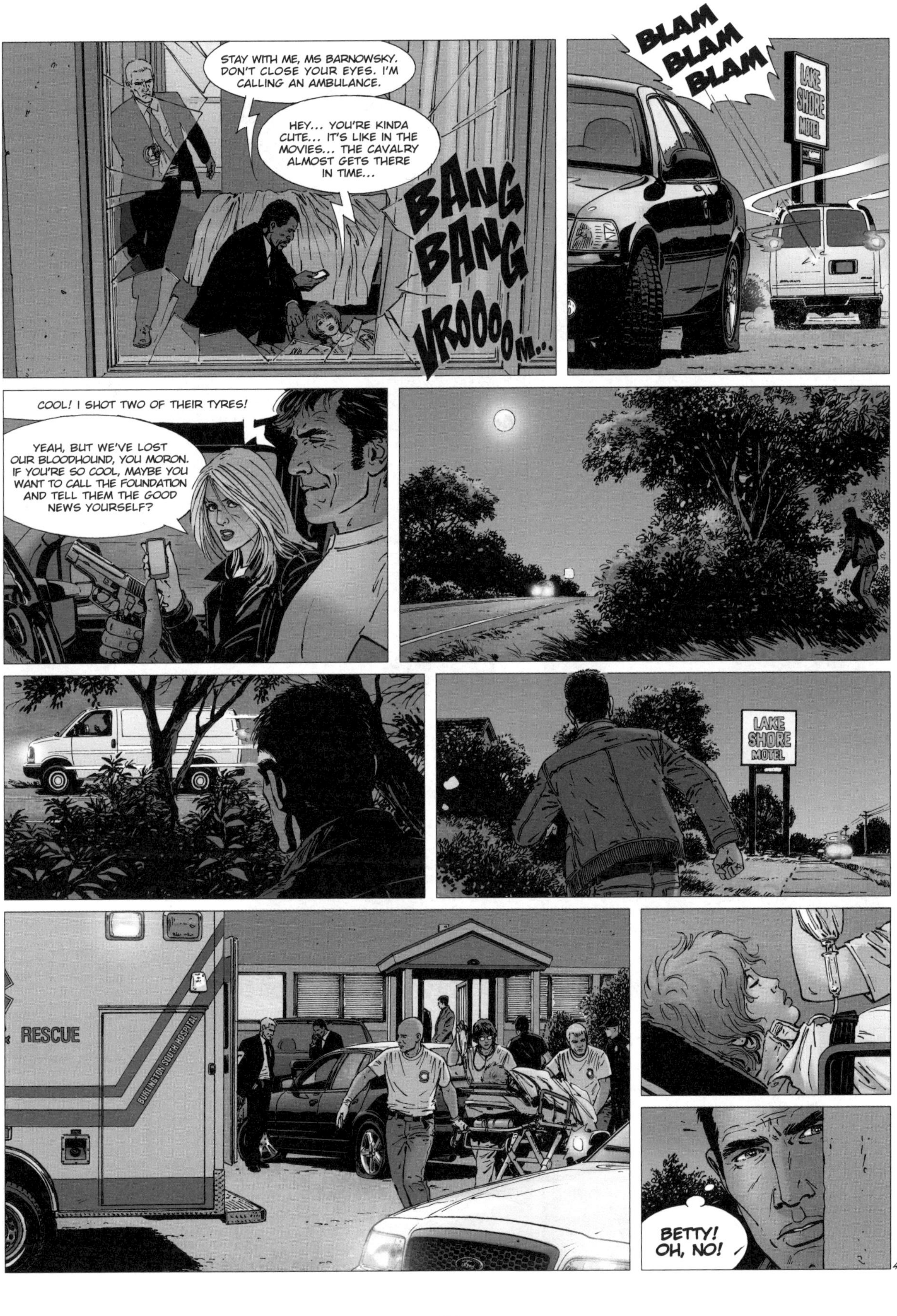
STAY WITH ME, MS BARNOWSKY. DON'T CLOSE YOUR EYES. I'M CALLING AN AMBULANCE.
HEY... YOU'RE KINDA CUTE... IT'S LIKE IN THE MOVIES... THE CAVALRY ALMOST GETS THERE IN TIME...
BANG BANG
VROOOOOM...
BLAM BLAM BLAM
LAKE SHORE MOTEL
COOL! I SHOT TWO OF THEIR TYRES!
YEAH, BUT WE'VE LOST OUR BLOODHOUND, YOU MORON. IF YOU'RE SO COOL, MAYBE YOU WANT TO CALL THE FOUNDATION AND TELL THEM THE GOOD NEWS YOURSELF?
LAKE SHORE MOTEL
RESCUE
BURLINGTON SOUTH HOSPITAL
BETTY! OH, NO!
45

THANKS TO JULIANNE AND MCLANE GOING TO ST ANDREWS, WE KNOW AT LEAST ONE PLACE OUR FUGITIVE HAS NO CHOICE BUT TO GO TO. WE'LL FIND HIM, MADAM.

YOU SEEM REMARKABLY SURE OF YOURSELF, MILDRED. WE'VE ALREADY PAID A STEEP ENOUGH PRICE TO KNOW THAT THIS MAN IS HIGHLY INTELLIGENT, WITH OR WITHOUT HIS MEMORIES...

WE'RE STILL HOLDING JONES AND CARRINGTON AS WILD CARDS. I CAN ACTIVATE THEM WITH A SINGLE ORDER FROM YOU, MADAM.

LITTLE JOE? HERB HERE. THE FBI JUST NOTIFIED ALL INVOLVED OFFICERS. BETTY BARNOWSKY WAS JUST ARRESTED... NO. SHE GOT PRETTY SHOT UP BY SOME FOLKS; THE NOTE DIDN'T SAY WHO... SHE'S IN CRITICAL CONDITION. THAT'S ALL I KNOW.

CALL ME BACK WHEN YOU HAVE THE HOSPITAL NAME AND ROOM NUMBER. AND HERB?... HURRY UP!

LA POSTE

Please put this memory card in your safe until Jason comes back.
I cannot wait to come home, sweet Armand. The good thing about going away is that it reminds you of how much you love the ones you're missing...

I can never thank you enough for loving me so well in return.
Betty

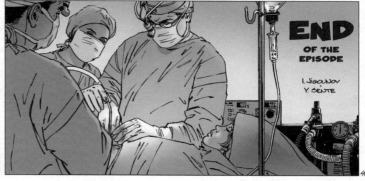

END
OF THE EPISODE

J. JIGOUNOV
Y. SENTE